Y0-AFY-395

Morning Has Broken

About the author
Richard Harries, who is Dean of King's College, London, was born in 1936 and educated at Selwyn College, Cambridge, and Cuddesdon Theological College. A priest of the Church of England, he has spent much of his ministry in parish life including six years in Hampstead and nine years as Vicar of Fulham (All Saints). He was on the staff of Wells Theological College and retains an interest in ordination training as Chairman of the Southwark Ordination Course. His main academic interests are the relationship between religion and literature and Christian Ethics. He has written widely on the ethics of war, revolution and the nuclear issue.

Mr Harries is the author of ten books, including *Prayer and the Pursuit of Happiness* and *Seasons of the Spirit* (with George Every and Kallistos Ware). He writes for a number of papers and journals including a weekly column for "The Church Times". He is also a regular contributor to Television and Radio, being best known for his BBC Radio 4 "Prayer for the Day", and "Thought for the Day" spots. In 1983 he was voted tenth in the BBC's "Man of the Year" competition.

Mr Harries is married to a doctor. They have two children, a son studying medicine at Cambridge and a daughter still at school.

Morning Has Broken

Thoughts and Prayers from
BBC Radio 4's 'Today' Programme

Richard Harries

Foreword by Brian Redhead

Marshalls

Marshalls Paperbacks
Marshall Pickering
3 Beggarwood Lane, Basingstoke,
Hants, RG23 7LP, UK
A subsidiary of the Zondervan Corporation Inc.

Copyright © 1985 by Richard Harries
First published by Marshall Morgan & Scott Ltd

All rights reserved. No part of this publication
may be reproduced, stored in a retrieval system,
or transmitted, in any form or by any means,
electronic, mechanical, photocopying, recording
or otherwise, without the prior permission of the
publisher.

ISBN 0 551 01178 5

Typeset by Alan Sutton Publishing Limited.
Printed in Great Britain by Hazell Watson &
Viney Ltd, Aylesbury, Bucks.

For those who listen to Radio 4
on Friday mornings

Books by Richard Harries

Prayers of Hope
Turning to Prayer
Prayers of Grief and Glory
Being a Christian
Should a Christian Support Guerillas?
Praying Round the Clock
The Authority of Divine Love
Seasons of the Spirit (with George Every
    and Kallistos Ware)
Prayer and the Pursuit of Happiness

Contributed to:

Stewards of the Mysteries of God, ed. E James
What Hope in an Armed World?, ed. R Harries
Unholy Warfare, ed. D Martin and P Mullen
The Cross and the Bomb, ed. F Bridger
Dropping the Bomb, ed. J Gladwyn

Contents

Foreword by Brian Redhead

He would appear in the studio just before a quarter to seven every Friday morning, plastic cup in one hand, neat script in the other. Sometimes he was in mufti but mostly in the clothes of his calling, with a grey stock, and a clerical collar, and a high-necked jacket that hinted of an earlier age. Rogue Harries, I would call him, but in truth he looked more like a wary Pimpernel with one ear cocked for the guillotine.

He would suffer the headlines and then launch forth. Timpers and I never had any doubts that he was the best at it. Every egg a bird, we would chortle, every bird a whistler, or words to that effect. His were, and are, homilies in the best sense, meant for the listener.

What I always enjoyed most was not only that they were lucid and serious, but that they – or rather Richard – wore his learning lightly. He talked of the past and of the people of the past and above all of poetry as if these recollections were part of the everyday conversation of thoughtful people. As indeed they are, or should be.

I never said this to his face, but in private I used to compare him with George Herbert. And then one day I was reading another of the great metaphysical poets, Henry Vaughan. That's Richard, I thought. His prayers glow with the true inner light, like Henry Vaughan's.

I know that they do, because at my own moment of greatest sorrow I found them a source of great comfort and strength.

You will too.

Thoughts and Feelings

Gracious Moments

It's nice when people write to me – sometimes, I must say, with some surprising requests. I once returned from holiday to find a letter asking me to confirm in writing that the thought of having an injection makes me feel faint – which it does – so I was happy to oblige. Over the years I have received some very moving letters; letters from *very* senior citizens in Old People's homes with friends gone, and senses failing, yet exuding faith and hope. Or widows who have 'come through', who, some years after bereavement, feel they have now restructured their lives, found peace, and are full of gratitude for the happy years they have had with their husbands.

It's strange, this instinct for gratitude, isn't it? Once when Katherine Mansfield saw a beautiful spot in the mountains she, a non-believer, said, 'If only one could make some small grasshoppery sound of praise to someone, of thanks to someone – but to who?'

This kind of instinct to say thanks – thanks for existence as such, whatever the circumstances – is not I think simply an echo of our parents telling us, 'Now say "Thank you"'. And though it can get distorted, as when people desperately look around to count their blessings because they are scared to look at the horrible side of life – it seems much more fundamental, more deep seated than that. The last poem W.H. Auden wrote before his death in 1972 listed some of the things for which he felt gratitude. It contains the line, 'Let your last thinks all be thanks'. And although there are some people who are congenital grumblers it is a never failing source of amazement how people succeed, not simply in struggling on but in doing just that – turning their thinks into thanks.

There is a poem by Elizabeth Jennings that I like. And in case anyone thinks the poem makes it sound all too easy I am sure Elizabeth Jennings won't mind my saying that she has had troubles enough in her life, including much illness. It's called, 'I count the moments'.

I count the moments of my mercies up,
I make a list of love and find it full.
I do all this before I fall asleep.
Others examine conscience. I tell
My beads of gracious moments shining still.
I count my good hours and they guide me well.

Heavenly Father,
grant us this day some gracious moments,
and at the end of the day
give us grace to see them shining still.

Anger

Anger of one kind or another is always in the news. But there is a great deal of anger *inside* most of us. What should we do with it?

First, the capacity to be angry is a thoroughly good thing. Anger is part of our nature and our nature, however spoilt, has been created good. It is part of the raw material of our personality and without the ability to feel angry at life's frustrations, it is difficult to see how human beings could have achieved anything at all.

Secondly, how we express our anger should be related to the kind of relationship we have with the other person. In principle, the closer the relationship the more appropriate it is that we should be fully known, angry warts and all. As so often Blake got it right 200 years ago when he said:

'I was angry with my friend
I told my wrath, my wrath did end.
I was angry with my foe
I told it not, my wrath did grow.'

With someone we don't like we tend to be coldly polite and our resentment festers inside us. With someone who cares for us it is often right to let our emotional hair down. So, if someone gets furious with you – take heart, it could be a compliment to your relationship with them! A sign that they think it can take the strain of that degree of emotional honesty.

Thirdly, we can express this anger to God. There is a great deal of anger in the Bible – sometimes, it seems, far too much, but whatever else we may think, it is at least emotionally real. As George Macdonald said: 'Complaint against God is far nearer to God than indifference about him'. It is above all in the psalms that human anger is brought before God. Sometimes the sentiments offend us but, as they say, all human life is there, including what we feel at life's many frustrations. The psalms bring human resentment and self-pity and sheer anger before God – which is why people throughout the ages have found them such a marvellous vehicle not only for our moments of happiness but for all those other feelings which we hardly dare to admit to ourselves but which we can admit to God. And sometimes, when we can honestly bring our wrath to God we can come through to a no less honest acceptance of life. In one of his poems, W.H.Auden let out a howl of rage that his friend did not return his love. He finds reasons enough, as he says:

'to face the sky and roar
to argue and despair'.

But he comes in the end to a realisation that whatever he feels, he is called, as he puts it, to 'Bless what there is for being'.

Heavenly Father,
You accept us as we are,
anger and all.
Help us to be real before you
that you may be real for us.

Fear

I suspect that almost everybody in the country relived in their own mind the story of how a farmworker, Mr. Roy Tapping, wrenched himself free from a bailing machine, picked up his severed arm and then staggered bloodily over 500 yards to the nearest farmhouse. We relive such incidents not only out of admiration for someone-else's bravery but because we imagine ourselves in such a situation. We wonder how we would have coped with it. And if you are anything like me, it brings out all sorts of fears and terrors.

Fear is, I suppose, one of the most basic constituents of our nature. We fear accident and illness. Every crash we read about sends a chill, reminds us that life is precarious, and we are vulnerable. We cover up of course. So Woody Allen, 'I'm not afraid of dying. I just don't want to be there when it happens.' But the fear is there. We fear what might happen and no less we fear how we might react to what might happen. What lack of courage, sheer cowardice might be revealed: it is doubts about our own moral and spiritual courage that often bother us most.

As someone who faints even at the thought of an injection, the only comfort I have is that some of the bravest men have been no less scared than the rest of us. Thomas More was a brave man if ever there was one. He went to his death joking with the executioner. Yet he wrote to his beloved daughter from the tower: 'Surely Meg, a fainter heart than thy frail father hath, canst thou not have . . . I am of nature so shrinking from pain, that I am almost afraid of a fillip. I have with a heavy, fearful heart, forecasting all such perils and painful deaths, often been lying long, restless and wakeful.'

Thomas More was aware of his fear. Yet that, by itself, is not enough, for fear can be crippling. I find it very interesting the way Jesus treats fear. In Luke's Gospel we read these words: 'I tell you, my friends, do not fear those who kill the body, and after that have no more that they can do. But I will warn you whom to fear: fear him who, after he has killed, has power to cast into hell; yes, I tell you, fear him. Are not five sparrows sold for two pennies? And not one of them is forgotten before God. Why even the hairs of your head are all numbered. Fear not; you are of more value than many sparrows.'

Some of that we find very shocking. Yet Jesus takes fear seriously – and says in effect: if you are fearful, what is the worst thing that can happen to you? To be shut up in ourselves, cut off from God, for ever and ever, which is hell. But though we should fear that, it is also true that in God fear is banished, for we are infinitely precious to Him. The very hairs of our head are numbered.

O God, you know we are often fearful.
Give us courage and deepen our trust.
You are a rock which nothing can shatter.
On you we can place the whole weight of our
lives.

The Unknown Future

In the summer of 1833 John Henry Newman was becalmed in the Mediterranean. He was desperately anxious to get back to England and worrying all the time about the state of the church. Moreover, as he kept finding himself saying: 'I have a work to do in England'. As he was becalmed, he wrote these lines:

> 'Lead, kindly Light, amid the encircling gloom,
> Lead thou me on;
> The night is dark, and I am far from home,
> Lead thou me on.'

These words have since become well known as a hymn and also one of Mother Theresa's favourite prayers.

There is one slightly incongrous line. 'I was not ever thus', wrote Newman, 'I loved the garish day'. It is difficult to imagine Newman, an austere, disciplined man, ever loving the garish day. Also, it must be admitted, that the hymn is not for every mood. It is perhaps best for a Sunday evening when one is feeling a touch melancholy: aware, like Newman, of the encircling gloom and that the night is dark.

The hymn has two well known lines which have made it of such practical importance for so many people over the last 150 years:

'Keep thou my feet; I do not ask to see
The distant scene; one step enough for me.'

I am sure you have been at meetings, as I have,
where a very important decision has to be made.
There are some good, sensible, rational arguments
about all the factors. Yet we cannot help thinking
that rational assessment can only take us so far. In
the end there are just so many unknown considera-
tions. This is true with so many of the decisions we
make. The future is unpredictable and with all the
computers in the world we still cannot calculate the
distant scene. And for the Christian, it is not simply
that the future is unknown, it is that God may have
a purpose beyond what we can grasp at the
moment. Sailing back to England in July 1833
Newman might have guessed that he had a large
part to play in the religious revival that sprang up
almost as he jumped ashore – the Oxford Movement. But he could not have predicted that only a
few years later, in 1845, he would have become a
Roman Catholic. And no one then could have
foreseen that the ideas he took into the Roman
Catholic Church sowed seeds that would flower in
our own time – for, as has often been said, the
Second Vatican Council saw nearly all Newman's
ideas – his emphasis on the laity for example –
which were not always accepted in his own time,
thoroughly vindicated. The mystery of Newman's
life is not essentially different from the mystery of
our own. Perhaps like him we have to learn to pray:

'Lord, Lead thou me on
Keep thou my feet; I do not ask to see
The distant scene; one step enough for me.'

Loneliness

Sister Martina, a speaker on the radio, admitted to the experience of loneliness. She said 'I walked by the canal one day feeling lonely.' I think she was rather brave. Most of us are not so open about such feelings. But if we open our eyes we can sometimes detect what is going on in the minds of others. In one of his poems R.S.Thomas describes a farmer walking down a lane and stopping to listen to a bird:

Wait a minute, wait a minute – four swift notes:
He turned, and it was nothing, only a thrush
In the thorn bushes easing its throat.
He swore at himself for paying heed,
The poor hill farmer, so often again
Stopping, staring, listening, in vain,
His ear betrayed by the heart's need.

Sister Martina went on to describe a brief encounter with a stranger which eased her sense of being alone. But, sometimes, our relationships with others, though they help for a bit, also accentuate the feeling of isolation. If someone close to you dies the one who is left will feel much more alone than they would have done if they had never been close to anyone. They have known, at least on occasion, what it is to make contact with another human being; and they therefore experience all that much more sharply the pain when that contact is no longer possible.

I think myself that some sense of isolation is inescapable; it is part of our lot as human beings. Much of the time it feels as though we are minds and hearts locked away from one another behind walls of flesh. Certainly that's how some modern writers seem to experience our condition today. In Samuel Beckett's writings, for example, we never move far away from the sense of a mind locked in upon itself; shut up with its own inner voices.

So, if this really is part of our lot, perhaps the first thing we are meant to do is face it. It's not easy. We would almost rather do anything else; and we do do almost anything else. It's said that some early Christian hermits, after about two or three weeks on their own in a cave would come rushing out looking for someone, anyone, to talk to. But unless we can face being on our own we will never make a true relationship with anyone else. Our contacts with others will be attempts to fill the hole inside us; they will sense it and be wary. Dietrich Bonhoeffer, who was killed for his resistance to Hitler, wrote, as a result of his attempt to build a community of Christians, a little book called *Life Together*. I think it is one of the best things he did. There he wrote 'Let him who cannot be alone beware of community. He will only do harm to himself and the community. Alone you stood before God when he called you; alone you had to answer that call; alone you had to struggle and pray; and alone you will die and give an account to God. You cannot escape from yourself; for God has singled you out.' Those words of Bonhoeffer indicate where our hope lies. For it is often in facing ourselves, the fact that I am I, a unique I, that we become dimly aware of one who is aware of us: who is present with us; who addresses us.

Lord, your presence

fills the universe,

fills the earth,

this room,

my mind.

Lord, I am still

before you

Failure

Jeremy Irons was interviewed by a newspaper and the subject got round to religion. Referring to his role in *Brideshead Revisited*, Jeremy Irons said 'I understand why Charles Ryder went for Catholicism. I haven't reached that state in my life where I've lost everything else. I'm not homeless, loveless, middle-aged.' I don't know how serious Jeremy Irons was being, but he does put into words what many people feel about religion. We turn to it as a compensation, when everything else in our lives has failed. And what are religious people meant to say about that? Fiercely deny it? Bitterly resent the implication? If we are wise I think we will admit the truth in it. Listen to how St. Paul addresses his readers. 'Not many of you were wise according to worldly standards, not many were powerful, not many were of noble birth; but God chose what is foolish, what is weak, what is low and despised.' Christians are no great shakes.

So, what can be said? First, it is a feature of all our experience that when things are going well it is easy to forget that there are many more important things in life than worldly success. For example, if you've always had lots of friends it is difficult to fully appreciate what it is to feel lonely. Secondly, sometimes, when we have been stripped down to nothing, we feel we have come up against the realities of life, the deeper realities. It is not just that people at rock bottom sometimes turn to God – they do, and he is the rock that is there for us at such times. As the hymn puts it:

When other helpers fail, and comforts flee,
Help of the helpless, O abide with me.

But even more basic than that, at times of grief or failure or rejection or injury, we are forced to go below the surface of our lives. The decoration, the gloss, the bunting are all swept away and we are face to face with the iron girders – our own courage and will to go on, and faith (and our lack of these things).

So should we wait then, as Jeremy Irons ironically suggested, until we are 'homeless, childless, middle-aged, loveless'. If we do, *we* are the losers. As the Priest said to the girl in Rose Macauley's novel, *The Towers of Trebizond*, 'Shall you come back, when it is taken out of your hands and it will cost you nothing? When you will have nothing to offer to God but a burnt-out fire and a fag end? Oh, he'll take it, he'll take anything we offer. It is you who will be impoverished for ever by so poor a gift'.

Heavenly Father,
We hold in your presence
those who lives seem to have little satisfaction,
those whom life has knocked,
that when other comforts flee
they may indeed know you to be the help of the
    helpless.
And we pray also
for those who have things going for them
who seem to be happy and successful
that they may be further enriched
by offering you out of their fullness.

Depression

The Reverend Sydney Smith was the greatest wit of his generation. He was also an exponent, as well as a practitioner, of no-nonsense, practical goodness. This down-to-earth quality comes across very well in the famous advice he gave to a friend on how to cope with depression. After beginning, 'Nobody has suffered more from low spirits than I have done, so I feel for you', he gave twenty recommendations some of which are: '4. Take short views of human life not farther than dinner or tea. 6. See as much as you can of those friends who respect and like you. 8. Make no secret of low spirits to your friends but talk of them fully: they are always the worse for dignified concealment. 9. Attend to the effects tea and coffee produce upon you. 11. Don't expect too much of human life, a sorry business at the best. 15. Make the room where you commonly sit gay and pleasant. 17. Don't be too severe upon yourself or underrate yourself. 18. Keep good blazing fires. 19. Be firm and constant in the exercise of rational religion.'

These twenty tips seem to me to be very sound as well as amusingly put. But recently I came across a rather different approach to this malaise. Philip Toynbee was a highly distinguished reviewer who, for two years before his death, kept a kind of spiritual diary. For after a lifetime in a spiritual scrubland he discovered, in a quite undramatic way, that he believed. He also realised that the depression, which had been with him for about seven years, was getting worse, indeed incapacitating him. He knew all the obvious causes. But as he writes in his journal, which has been reprinted as a paperback, 'I gradually began to think of this depression in a quite new set of terms. Instead of looking for its causes and thinking about how to get rid of them, I began to look for its purpose and to wonder how I could fulfill them.'

In fact, the first step he took was to persuade his doctor to get him ECT, which helped the depression to lift. But he still felt there was some purpose in it, though as he wrote, 'I couldn't and still can't tell whether God sends us such acute afflictions to bring us to some new understanding through our pain.' That's right. But it may be that if, under God, our unconscious is feeling its way to a new, different life, and our conscious mind for some reason is stopping the breakthrough, the result may be a kind of depression. Anyway, the turning point for Philip Toynbee was when he tried to see some purpose in the depression and to fulfill it. As he wrote, 'I am now as sure as I can be that depression is often a sign, whether human or divine, that the life of the victim needs to be drastically changed; that acts of genuine contrition are called for; that the dark block within can be dissolved only by recognising that something like an inner death and resurrection is demanded of the sufferer.'

His experience may not be applicable to

anyone else, but his attempt to see a purpose in what happened to him – a life-giving purpose – was a turning point for him and is suggestive for us.

Grant O God, that in all the circumstances of
    our lives,
however dark,
we may discern some light,
That from all the ills that beset us
We may draw some good.

People

St Teresa of Avila

At the time the Mary Rose set sail, unknown to those who watched her, there was living in Spain one of the most remarkable women the world has known: Teresa of Avila, who died on 15th October 1582. If you are one of those people who can't spell or punctuate you will feel some sympathy for her, neither could she. Yet she wrote books that have become classics because she wrote as she spoke, in a direct, vigorous and humorous manner that has always appealed to people. You may know what she said, after much personal suffering, to God. 'If this is how you treat your friends, no wonder you have so few.'

Again, if you are someone who feels that life only begins in middle age you will feel some kinship with her. It was only at the age of forty, after what she called her second conversion, that she got down to the Christian life in earnest. There is a passage in her book *The Interior Castle* which I'm sure must refer to her own period of drifting. 'Though we may still be engaged in the amusements and vanities of this world, yet such are the pity and compassion of the Lord of ours, so desirous is he that we should love him and seek his company, that in one way or another he never ceases calling us to him.'

Teresa had a series of remarkable spiritual experiences. 'Once when I was at prayer' she wrote 'I saw for a brief moment, without distinctness of form but with complete clarity, how all things are seen in God and how He contains all things within Him.' Yet she remained an extremely shrewd and practical woman, what the Americans would call an achiever. She decided to reform her religious order and founded seventeen new convents, raising the money and giving them a sound start. She was the kind of person who in our time could easily take over an ailing business and transform its fortunes, then buy up more companies and put in good managers on the same principles that she selected nuns. There must be no spiritual passengers; each one must be fit to be a prioress. Yet it is for her inner life that she will always be remembered and revered. She had powerful religious experiences; but perhaps more important than this is the careful teaching on prayer that she gave to others, and above all, the wholeheartedness of her commitment. She was totally given over to God in a way which few of us desire, let alone emulate. For her, God was an ever present reality and she conveys to us half-hearted, half-believing folk, four hundred years later in a very different culture, something of that reality.

Here are some words St Teresa wrote on her bookmark, words which must often have helped her find an inner serenity in the midst of her busy outward life.

Let nothing disturb thee;
Nothing afright thee.
All things are passing;
God never changeth.
Patient endurance attaineth to all things;
Whom God possesseth in nothing is wanting.
Alone God sufficeth.

Lancelot Andrews

Millions and millions of people have lived on this earth. Whom should we remember and why? On September 25th, 1626, Lancelot Andrews died. Is he worth remembering? He was a famous preacher. As a contemporary put it on one occasion 'The Bishop of Ely preached at court on Christmas Day to great applause'. The king was so moved he asked for the sermon notes to put under his pillow. But I must confess that whenever I have tried to read the sermons I've found them heavy going.

Lancelot Andrews was also a well-known scholar. His parents were probably what we would call poor but honest. Amongst the things he thanked God for was the fact that he was not 'a sorry egg of a sorry crow'. He was a scholarship boy, ending up as Master of his college at Cambridge and speaking 17 languages. His influence in this sphere continues for he was chairman of one of the panels that produced the King James Version of the bible and T.S.Eliot admired him so much he incorporated some of his lines into one of his best known poems. But is this enough to make him especially worth remembering? He was a good churchman of course. Bishop of a number of Dioceses and of special importance to the Anglican Church, which is why they have a special day for him. But this itself would hardly give him universal appeal. So let me get to the heart of the matter.

He was a good man. The continental scholar Casaubon said 'No words can express what true piety, what uprightness of judgement I find in him'. But Andrews wasn't stuffy. He had wide sympathies, giving very generously to those in need, and I like the understanding he showed when a portly alderman came to him for advice because he kept falling asleep in the afternoon sermon. 'Eat less dinner' suggested Andrews. But still the man fell asleep, so he came back. 'Take your dinner earlier' said Andrews, 'eat as much as you want, have a good nap and then go to church'. Rather more dangerous was the occasion when King James asked Lancelot Andrews and his friend Bishop Neil if he might take his subjects' money without all the fuss and formality of parliament. 'God forbid Sir', said Neil, but you should, you are the breath of our nostrils'. Andrews was quiet at first but when pressed replied 'Sir, I think it is lawful for you to take my brother Neil's money because he offers it.'

Preacher, scholar, churchman, a likeable human being but above all a good man. And this goodness was rooted in prayer, which was at the heart of his life. He wrote his own prayers, culled from phrases from the Bible and the early church fathers, and collected them in a notebook. He was a very methodical person and he had special prayers for each day of the week and each time of prayer contained its own acts of praise and penitence and intercessions. This is part of one of his morning prayers:

Glory be to Thee, O Lord, glory to Thee
Creator of light,
and enlightener of the world.
Thou who didst create the Visible light,
The sun's rays, a flame of fire
day and night, evening and morning.
Thou who didst create the light invisible,
The light that never sets,
that which may be known of God, the law
    written in the heart. . . .

George Herbert

George Herbert died just over 350 years ago – on February 27th 1633. For many people he is their favourite poet. He was a highly talented young man, fluent in many languages, and he was appointed Public Orator to the University of Cambridge. Here he quickly came to the notice of influential patrons, including the king, James 1st. Then they all died – and George Herbert thought about putting his courtesy, charm and verbal skills at the service of the King of Kings. It was a struggle, for he was ambitious. Also his friends thought it beneath the dignity of a man of his aristocratic birth and abilities to become a priest. But as George Herbert replied to one such, 'It hath been formerly ajudged that the domestic servants of the King of Heaven should be of the noblest families on earth; and though the iniquity of late times have made clergymen meanly valued, and the sacred name of priest contemptible, yet I will labour to make it honourable by consecrating all my learning, and all my poor abilities, to advance the glory of that God that gave them.'

So after much heart searching and with a heavy sense of his responsibility to the four hundred souls in the village, George Herbert became parish priest of Bemerton near Salisbury. Here, in his writing and his life, he set out the ideal of the country priest to which every country parson has since aspired. In his long poem *The Porch* he gives himself much sound advice, his wit turning ordinary moral maxims into something interesting. He deals with every aspect of social life from hogging the conversation at table to making jokes at other people's expense. Here, for example, is what he says about drink:

> Drink not the third glass, which thou canst not
> tame,
> When once it is within thee; but before
> Mayst rule it, as thou list; and poure the shame
> Which it would poure on thee, upon the floore.
> It is most just to throw that on the ground,
> Which would throw me there, if I keep the
> round.

George Herbert was highly musical and his poems are musical in their effect. But they are just as much prayers, prayers of struggle and anguish with the God he often felt to be absent. Some have become well-known as hymns; his version of Psalm 23, 'The King of Love my Shepherd is', 'Teach me my God in all things thee to see' and 'Let all the world, in every corner sing', for example. It is their human quality as well as the faith in them that appeals to people.

Prayer was at the heart of Herbert's life. 'Resort to Sermons', he said, 'but to prayers most: Praying's the end of preaching.'

This is part of his fine poem on prayer:

Prayer the churches banquet, Angels age,
    God's breath in man returning to his birth,
    The soul in paraphrase, heart in pilgrimage,
A kind of tune, which all things heare and fear;
Softnesses, and peace, and joy, and love, and
    blisse,
    Exalted Manna, gladnesse of the best,
    Heaven in ordinarie, man well drest,
The milkie way, the bird of Paradise,
    Church-bells beyond the starres heard, the
    souls bloud,
    The land of spices; something understood.

William Wilberforce

William Wilberforce died on 29th July 1833 and the Church of England now keeps 29th July as a permanent memorial to him. Wilberforce was born with many natural advantages. His family was rich, with money made from trade to the Baltic and if you go to Hull you can still see his house. He was a natural orator. 'Of all the men I know,' said his friend Pitt, 'Wilberforce has the greatest natural eloquence.' Above all he had charm and a naturally pleasing personality. People spoke of his vivacity, his delight in little things. 'I have always heard' said Madame de Stael, 'that he was the most religious, but now I find he is the wittiest man in England.' Wilberforce once told a missionary meeting that he had had a dream that he was in hell – 'It was just like here,' he added, almost to himself, 'I could not get the near the fire for parsons.'

Wilberforce had a natural love of pleasure and with his ability he could have done almost anything he wanted with his life. In fact, he was converted to a more serious and personal understanding of Christianity and instead of a life of pleasure, he chose public service; and instead of great office, he chose a great cause. He gave his whole life first to the abolition of the slave traffic and then to the abolition of slavery in the British Empire. The vested interests were large, the opposition formidable, but three days before he died word came that his life's work had succeeded.

Inevitably during this century, Wilberforce's reputation has fluctuated. Historians have accused him of supporting liberal causes abroad and opposing them at home; they have pointed to economic rather than moral factors as the determining cause in the abolition of slavery and so on. Yet as a recent biographer, Ian Bradley, has written: 'It is still the saintliness of Wilberforce that shines out . . . a life full of fun and gaiety and never over-pious or sanctimonious.' There is still enough goodness in his character to think of him as his contemporaries did, as 'The Saint'. One particular example remains in my mind. Wilberforce's eldest son could never stick at anything and in a disastrous business venture lost nearly all his father's money. Wilberforce had to sell his house and live with his other children. He took it all without a trace of bitterness or recrimination, counting his blessings as always. He said about it all: 'It has only increased my happiness, for I have in consequence been spending the winter with one of my other sons.' Towards the end of Wilberforce's life, a friend wrote of him: 'I wish you could have seen him as he stood under the Tulip tree telling of many of whom he has seen pass – 'and they are gone, and here am I', he said, 'a wreck left for the next tide – but yet abounding in blessings and enjoyments".

We give you thanks for our creation
    and all the blessings of this life,
Especially the blessing of good men made Holy.

Raoul Wallenberg

When the history of the 20th century comes to be
written one name will flash one like a lighthouse
in the surrounding darkness – Rauol Wallenberg,
who in 1982 may or may not have celebrated his
70th birthday on this earth. For there is a mystery
about him. He may still be alive. In Budapest in
1945 he was taken into custody by the Russians.
At first they denied all knowledge of him. Then
in 1957 they did admit that they had taken him
prisoner but said that he had died in prison. Since
then however many people have claimed to have
seen him in prison camps in Russia, the latest
claim being in 1975. Yet, whether he is alive or
dead now is not perhaps so important as what he
did in saving the lives of Jews in the last year of
the war. For this he was made an honorary
citizen of the United States, an honour he shares
with only one other person, Sir Winston Churchill.

Raoul Wallenberg came from an aristocratic
Swedish family and like many young men his life
was fairly directionless until he was asked to go
in July 1944 on a special mission to Budapest.
Many Hungarians were co-operating with Nazi
Germany and Jews were being put to death by
the thousand. Wallenberg's job, under the cover
of his status as a Swedish diplomat, was to do
what he could to save some of them. He repeat-

edly confronted SS commanders taking Jews away to be murdered and claimed that they were Swedish citizens. As a result when Soviet forces took Budapest a few months later, about 120,000 Jews were still alive, by far the largest community of Jewish origin remaining in East Europe at the end of the Second World War. He gave direct protection to 20,000 through giving them special protective passports and through his initiative and example, another 100,000 were saved. All this through what has been called a combination of reckless heroism and subtle diplomacy.

The following account is typical of the stories told by those who survived as a result of his action. Wallenberg once drove to the station where he learned that a train load of Jews was about to leave for Auschwitz. The young SS officer supervising the transport ordered him off the platform. Wallenberg brushed him aside. 'Then he climbed up on the roof of the train and began handing in protective passes through the doors which had not yet been sealed. He ignored orders from the Germans for him to get down, then they began shooting at him, firing over his head. He ignored them and calmly continued handing out passports to the hands that were reaching out for them . . . After Wallenberg had handed over the last of the passports he ordered all those who had one to leave the train and walk to a caravan of cars parked nearby, all marked in Swedish colours. I don't remember exactly how many, but he saved dozens off that train, and the Germans were so dumbfounded they let him get away with it.'

Thank you God
for those who shine like a light in our darkness
those who reveal the potential in each one of us
those who give us the courage and confidence to
    act for good.

Martin Niemoller

One of the greatest men of the 20th century, who died in 1984 aged 92 was Martin Niemoller. During the First World War he was a U-boat commander and much decorated for his exploits. Characteristically in 1918 he refused to surrender his U-boat to the British. After the war he became ordained, wrote a best-seller, 'From U-boat to pulpit', attracted big crowds and seemed all set for a steady life in the church. Then the Nazis started to spread their poison, forming the German Christian Movement, with its deadly mixture of Nazi and Christian ideas. Niemoller saw what was happening and in 1933 formed the Pastors Emergency League from which sprang the Confessing church pledged to total opposition to Hitler's ideas. Despite an order from Hitler forbidding him to do so, Niemoller preached a series of courageous sermons and in 1937 was arrested on a charge of 'malicious attacks against the state'. He spent eight years in prison, usually in solitary confinement. After the Second War Niemoller was again active and controversial, opposing many of the policies of his government, particularly after he was converted to pacifism in 1954.

Niemoller's life reflects so much of the anguish of our century – and one of its central dilemmas: the relationship of the individual conscience to the state. And although, thank God, we have been spared the extreme choices presented to the German people, it is a problem that is always with us. The Government, this government or any other, must take what steps it considers necessary to safeguard national security. But equally, the individual conscience must always be vigilant and alert to what is going on. For there is a higher loyalty than that to the state. Under normal circumstances the state, according to the New Testament, is a divine Institution. It exists, as it were, under the providence of God, for our benefit. And it has nearly always been regarded as a legitimate vocation to serve the state – which is just as well, as millions of us do, as postmen and policemen, soldiers and stationmasters, tax men and hospital porters. Yet, as the life of Martin Niemoller reminds us, circumstances can arrise when laws have to be opposed in the name of a higher loyalty – and worse than that, a state can actually become demonic, as it did under Hitler in Nazi Germany, when of course it ceases to have any claim upon us.

Niemoller's conscience was as alert as anyone's in the 20th century. Yet after the Second World War he wanted to take his share of the guilt he felt all Christians in Germany shared. He wrote words which have since become famous: 'First they came for the Jews. I was silent. I was not a Jew. Then they came for the Communists. I was silent. I was not a Communist. Then they came for the trade unionists. I was silent. I was not a trade unionist. Then they came for me. There was no one left to speak for me.'

We give you thanks, O God, for those in our time who have recognised evil and had the courage to resist it. Keep our consciences alert and our minds vigilant.

Solzhenitsyn

When Solzhenitsyn was in London I had the great privilege of hearing him speak. What a witness to the capacity of the human spirit to survive! After the war, in which he was twice decorated for bravery, he was arrested and spent 8 years in a work camp and then 3 years in exile in Siberia. He was then diagnosed as having a cancer which was inoperable and incurable. Since then he has had to survive – with his spirit intact – in two very different worlds. In the Soviet Union as a famous writer opposed to the system – and in the West as a celebrity who could be made use of by the system. It is above all his fierce integrity that comes across. His novels have the same quality of simple, unadorned truth-telling as those of Tolstoy; and he is totally uncompromising in his critique of both Marxism and Western Materialism. Then, like so many Russians, and Dostoevsky in particular, he has this willingness to go to the heart of the matter. The key chapter in his novel *Cancer Ward* is called 'What men live by'.

He has made it quite clear what he himself lives by. He recalls a remark made to him as a child by older people trying to account for the disaster that had overtaken them: 'Men have forgotten God; that's why all this has happened' All that has happened now includes the suffering of the Soviet Union since then, the First World War and the materialism of the Western world. 'If I were called upon to identify the principal trait of the entire twentieth century', he has said, 'I would be unable to find anything more precise than to repeat once again – "Men have forgotten God"'.

Solzhenitsyn's theme, if it came from anyone else, would be easy to shut ones ears to. He says many things we just don't want to hear. But coming from him, one is forced to listen, to take seriously what he says, to allow oneself and all ones assumptions to be questioned. Some people find him too sombre. Yet twice I saw the prophetic, bearded face irradiated with a warm, lovely smile. And the Archbishop of Canterbury who has had him to supper told me he was the most marvellous company. Yet Solzhenitsyn makes it absolutely clear that this hope, this brightness he has within him, has a supernatural source; and though full of foreboding about the future of the world, he offers one way out. Instead of the ill-advised hopes of the last two centuries, which have reduced us to insignificance and brought us to the brink of nuclear and non-nuclear death, he says, 'We can only reach with determination for the warm hand of God, which we have so rashly and self-confidently pushed away.' Here is a prayer of Solzhenitsyn himself that I am very fond of because of its expression of total faith in God.

How easy it is for me to live with you, Lord!
How easy it is for me to believe in you!
When my mind is distraught and my reason
    fails,

when the cleverest people do not see further
than this evening and do not know
what must be done tomorrow –
you grant me the clear confidence
that you exist and that you will
take care
that all the ways of goodness are
not stopped.

And you will enable me to go on doing
as much as needs to be done.
And is so far as I do not manage it –
that means that you have allotted the task to
others

John Betjeman

Many people were saddened when John Betjeman died. For through his radio and television broadcasts he won the affection of millions. I think there were two reasons for this. First, his infectious enthusiasm for what interested him. There is a kind of Englishman, Charles Darwin was another, who does badly at university and who seems to have no particular talents, but who gets passionately interested in something. John Betjeman got passionately interested in churches, including Victorian churches, and made a whole life sharing his personal enthusiasm with us. In so far as we now appreciate the Victorians a little better, we owe it to him. In so far as we are tempted to pop into country churches when we are on holiday, and many millions do, it must be largely due to him.

Secondly, he shared all his fears and failings with us in his poetry. He faced up, as few of us do, to his most painful emotions. As in that poem of himself as a young boy leaving a tea party, which ends up:

> the words I heard my hostess's mother
>   employ
> to a guest departing, would ever diminish my
>   joy,

I wonder where Julia found that strange, rather common little boy?

His poems have melancholy moments most notably in 'The Cottage Hospital':

Say in what Cottage Hospital
whose pale green walls resound
With the tap upon polished parquet
of inflexible nurses' feet
Shall I myself be lying
when they range the screens around?

It was the combination of these two qualities, his zest for things and his shared fears, that made him most gloriously himself; and it was as himself he won our hearts, and God's too we trust and pray.

For John Betjeman was that rare person – someone who remained a most devout Anglican when all his fashionable friends fell into indifference or were converted to Roman Catholicism. And, something even rarer, he showed how it is possible to be both a devout Christian and gloriously oneself. There is a saying attributed to the Rabbi Susya: 'At the judgement they will not say to you, why were you not Moses, but why were you not Susya?' John Betjeman helped me to realise the truth of that. In one of his less well known poems he describes going into a Lincolnshire church and discovering an Indian there:

He stood in that lowering sunlight,
An Indian Christian priest
And why he was here in Lincolnshire
I neither asked nor knew

He then reflects on the mystery of the two
continents and the one God:

There where the white light flickers,
Here, as the rains descend,
The same mysterious Godhead
is welcoming his friend.

May that same mysterious Godhead, who
    welcomes us all as friends,
    bless us and keep us.

Faith and Hope

The Beauty of God

In *Brideshead Revisited* Charles Ryder queried his friend's beliefs:

'But my dear Sebastian, you can't seriously *believe* it all.'

'Can't I?'

'I mean about Christmas and the star and the three kings and the ox and the ass.'

'Oh yes, I believe that. It's a lovely idea.'

'But you can't *believe* things because they're a lovely idea.'

'But I *do*. That's how I believe.'

A large part of us will agree with Charles. Fairy stories may be lovely – but we don't for that reason believe in them, in the way we might put our trust in God. But there is something to be said for Sebastian's point of view and I would like to say it. First, God is beauty as well as truth and goodness. We are used to the connection between religion and morality – 'You, therefore, must be perfect, as your heavenly Father is perfect' said Jesus. But God is also the source and standard of all that is lovely. As St Augustine prayed, 'Oh Thou beauty most ancient and withall so fresh.'

Second, how do we come to give our allegiance to someone? It is because we are drawn to them. Something about their personality attracts us. So it is with God. Catching some glimpse of his lowly, vulnerable tender approach to us in Christ we want to respond. The Bible several times talks of

'The beauty of holiness' – that holiness in God draws us like holiday-makers to a sunset.

Third, whether or not you think the Christian faith is true, I wonder if you would or would not agree that it is the most beautiful idea that has ever been conceived? This is a God who because his nature is love, creates beings like himself who are genuinely free and who gives us a period on earth to develop as persons. Who, for love of us, becomes incarnate; unites himself with human life, sharing our human anguish to the full, that he may make us more Godlike and so ready for an eternal existence with the whole company of Heaven.

So, I would like to suggest that there is a parallel between reading a poem or novel and growing in faith. When we read a good novel it grips us and it will alter the way we see and feel about life. In the same way the Christian story can take hold of us and change us – as we enter into the world of a novel, so we can enter into the Christian world – that is, this world seen in a fresh perspective.

I'm not saying that because a story is lovely it necessarily has true things to say about ultimate reality. But what I do want to suggest, and this I think is what Sebastian meant in *Brideshead Revisited*, is that the compelling beauty of the Christian story can be a way into belief.

> Lord of beauty, thine the splendour
>   Shewn in earth and sky and sea,
> Burning sun and moonlight tender,
>   Hill and river, flower and tree:
> Lest we fail our praise to render
>   Touch our eyes that they may see.

The Awe and Horror of Nature

Perhaps like me you are one of the 10.6 million people who watched David Attenborough's TV series *The Living Planet*. And perhaps like me you were at once enthralled and horrified by the bits of nature we were shown. Two images remain in my mind. First, the male penguin which stands for three months of the year by icy seas carefully guarding the single egg balanced on its feet. Whilst the female disappears to look for food the male stands there, virtually still, in the freezing cold, with nothing to eat for month after month. What amazing care for that one precious egg! How incredibly strong is the drive to produce offspring and survive as a species. The other image is less happy. A caterpillar that is liable to be eaten to death by ants if they can get hold of it. So to protect himself he produces a resin which he dabs on the eyes of the marauding ants. This disorientates them, so they stagger about and it sets up such a strange smell that when the ant returns home its fellow ants think it is an enemy and eat it to death. What cruel vengeance, we cannot help thinking, a cruelty that is built into nature in so many ways. This, for many people, is the major stumbling blocks to any belief that behind nature is a loving God.

What can be said? First, at least, that animals do not anticipate their doom. We are fearful about what might happen to us. Animals don't think ahead. Then, although this does not apply to dogs, cats and horses and the more developed species, it seems that the lower animals anyway do not feel pain. The butterfly flutters about – then in a flash it is gone, eaten by some bird or insect; but it did not know it was about to go and the process of going, so far as we know, was not painful. Whilst it fluttered about flashing its colours in the sun it glorified God after its kind. It was itself; it lived the form of life for which God made it. So, something can be said. yet the cumulative effect of nature 'red in tooth and claw' is undoubtably distressing. And it was this, not the theory of evolution as such, which eroded Darwin's religious faith. 'Eat and be eaten' seems to be the pattern of nature and the creator of such a system seems to us to be inhuman. Yet, perhaps, there is a warning here not to think in purely human terms about God. William Blake once wrote:

Tiger! Tiger! burning bright
In the forests of the night!
What immortal hand or eye
Could frame thy fearful symmetry?

Lines which remind us of the awesomeness of nature. We think humanly but God thinks not only humanly but tigerly, and birdly, and snakely, and in thinking these creatures he thinks them into existence. There are dimensions of God reflected in the grandeur and wonder and fearsomeness of nature that our tiny minds cannot get round. Yet, we are not left without something to hold onto.

For, to us, God has revealed himself *humanly*. In Christ the mists of mystery part and we see the human face of God. We are human and God relates to us humanly.

We bless your holy name, O God,
for the mystery and awesomeness of animal life
but above all for the fact that in Christ
You meet us as one of us.

Falling Apples

One of the minor pleasures of Autumn are the
apples. A decent English apple still takes a lot of
beating. Yet we don't derive nearly as much
pleasure from our apples as did our grandparents.
In the last part of the 19th century hundreds of
varieties were known and people were often as
discriminating about their Blenheims and Pippins
as they were about their wine.

'So when the woman saw that the tree was good
for food, and that it was a delight to the eyes, and
that the tree was to be desired to make one wise,
she took of its fruit and ate; she also gave to her
husband and he ate. Then the eyes of both were
opened.' I wonder what variety that was? Perhaps
not an apple at all, though that is what Christian
art has always taken it to be. The human race
became conscious – our eyes have been opened –
we can know what we are doing, including know-
ing good and evil.

Its a mighty puzzling story and I don't pretend
to understand it: but the Christian church has
always found in it some valuable insights. I suppose the most obvious of these is that our growth
into consciousness, into knowledge, is always a
mixed blessing. William Golding brought this out
superbly in his own favourite novel, *The Inher-
itors*, about two groups of people at the dawn of
consciousness. One tribe is characterised by a

kindly innocence. The other has discovered fire and how to cross rivers – and also alcohol, murders and orgies. We have discovered drugs to cure people, heart operations, kidney transplants – and also chemical and bacteriological weapons. We have discovered how to blast tunnels through mountains and also how to blast one another off the face of the earth. In the 19th century most people were taken in by the myth of progress, the idea that life is getting better and better. Against that comforting illusion, the garden of Eden story warns us that eating the apple of knowledge is always as much a fall as it is a rise.

Yet, in our time, the opposite danger is present: the fear that things are getting worse and worse, leading inevitably to some new disaster. So the Christian church has always insisted that nothing that happens, nothing, can happen outside God's providence. However far we fall, we cannot fall outside his care. Moreover, within that providence he is always working to bring some new good out of each new evil. So Christian writers have usually had mixed feelings about the fall – they have not seen it as a total catastrophe. As that delightful Medieval carol put it:

Ne had the apple taken been,
The apple taken been,
Ne had never our lady
Abeen heavene queen.
Blessed be the time
That apple taken was,
Therefore we moun singen
Deo gracias.

St Paul dwelt wonderingly on this theme; and so did Julian of Norwich, who wrote:

> 'We need to fall, and we need to see that we have done so. For if we never fall we should not know how weak and pitiable we are in ourselves. Nor should we fully know the wonderful love of our Maker.'

Heavenly Father,
Into your hands we commend this day,
Grant that we may keep close to you,
And if we should fall away,
Make it the occasion for us to draw closer still.

Solidarity of Prayer

I don't know whether you would agree but I think that as a race the British are rather shy of talking about religion. We feel that our religion, whatever it is, is something very precious and private; and that to talk about it, except in special circumstances, such as to a priest or a close friend, somehow spoils it: makes it seem trivial or vulgar.

One result of this is that we look around for words that disguise what we really want to say. A friend is going into hospital, so you say to them, 'I'll be thinking of you' when you know, and they know, that if you are capable of prayer at all you really mean 'I'll be praying for you.' But it sounds a bit pious to say that; something only really holy people seem to be able to get away with! Besides, I have heard, 'I'll pray for you' uttered more as a threat than a promise – as though having lost the argument the person is turning to God to cudgel you into submission – and one is tempted to respond 'I'd rather you didn't'. Yet what, after all, could be more moving, than to know that others are sincerely praying for us? Normally when we relate to people our motives are so mixed; but when we pray for them we are trying to desire their good as God desires their good. T.S. Eliot has a haunting line, 'The purification of the motive in the ground of our beseeching.' Prayer purifies, for through prayer we come to want

God's good for the person we are fond of. So prayer is the highest form of caring. Of course I don't mean prayer instead of all the other things we ought to be doing. But prayer is the purest form of care and it purifies all our caring.

If there is anything more moving than someone saying, with authenticity, 'You'll be in my prayers', it is when they ask for our prayers. Often this too is hidden beneath a jocular front. 'Say one for me padre'. But it is half meant; and it brings out, as perhaps nothing else does, our dependence on one another. There is a similar sense of belonging together when the priest at the end of confession says to the penitent, 'Pray for me, a sinner'. The unions often express the most important moral value that the Trade Union movement cherishes – solidarity. But there is a deeper solidarity than any kind of action. The Orthodox call it sobornost; the fellowship of the Holy Spirit; the solidarity of prayer.

So prayer is not only the highest gift we can offer. It leads us into a profound uinity with one another.

Heavenly Father,
  We hold in your presence all those known to us who are ill or unhappy,
    those who mourn or are in any kind of distress.
Grant them the comfort of your presence.

What's the Point?

I was haunted by the story of Mr George Meegan from Rainham in Kent who completed a 19,000 mile walk from the tip of South America to the North of Alaska. He started walking in January 1977 and on the way got married and had two children. It's extraordinary isn't it, the tasks we set ourselves? People give years of their lives to be the first person to eat 400 oysters in half an hour or flip a tiddly wink 40 yards or dance non-stop for fifteen days. These, by the way, are made up, so don't take them as a challenge, but the *Guinness Book of Records* has pages of even more bizarre stuff.

It has been said, rightly I think, that man is a goal-seeking animal. And when we have completed one goal and have not yet set ourselves another, we can feel very lost. Mr Meegan was asked how he felt after his 19,000 mile walk, and he replied, 'I thought, oh my God, it's over. The end of my dreams. It was a terribly sad experience – it was a bereavement.' Studies of prisoners of war have shown that if they had someone to live for, a wife or child, they were likely to survive the experience. But if they were told that their family had been killed in a bombing raid, as they were sometimes out of sheer maliciousness, their will to survive collapsed. It's no wonder that people who retire, if they have lived for work for forty years, sometimes feel a similar sense of collapse.

We can look at this need to find goals in two ways. It can be seen simply as a device to help us through. The rest of the animal creation seems content not to find goals, cows chew the cud, cats sleep in the sun, dogs bound about. But whatever people say, we are not content simply to spend seventy years eating, sleeping or lying in the sun. We are restless; we need a purposive existence. And so to assuage our restlessness, we set ourselves tasks, sometimes the most extraordinary ones. Or we can regard this goal seeking not simply as a device to get us through life, but as a proper part of our nature, because there is an ultimate goal for which we are made, and all these other goals are simply first steps or false starts in that direction. There is one goal that is always before us, for God being infinite, there is literally no end to the horizons of knowledge and love that open out before us. Yet at the same time this is a goal that is utterly satisfying for even to seek is to touch that for which we are made. St Bernard of Clairvaux put it well when he wrote, 'But here is a paradox, that no one can seek the Lord who has not already found him', and added this prayer:

'It is thy will, O God to be found
that thou mayest more truly be sought,
to be sought that thou mayest
the more truly be found.'

70

Dying Into Happiness

I once took a group of students to visit St Christopher's Hospice, in South London, which has pioneered care for the terminally ill. It is a marvellous place and it has had a remarkable influence. If I ask myself what scares me most about dying, it's the thought of pain. And that, apparently, is how everyone feels. Nearly all the patients at St Christopher's say that it is not death but dying that they are frightened of. So that sets the first priority, keeping people out of pain. The trick as I understand it is very simple in theory, however much good judgement it requires in practice. Most of us wait until we feel the pain before we take anything for it. We get a headache so take an aspirin. In modern terminal care people are put on regular four hourly doses of drugs. They receive a new dose before the effect of the old one has completely worn off.

Secondly, I want to die in a caring atmosphere. Alas, this cannot be laid on as easily as drugs. But it helps if there are plenty of people around to do the work, and talk to the patients when they want it. St Christopher's has a good staff/patient ratio. We ought to be able to feel confident about every hospital in the country that there are enough staff available to give those who are dying the attention they need.

Thirdly, I want some Christian encouragement. Odd as it may seem, it is sometimes the clergy who are most diffident about making claims for the importance of religion. But anyone with any faith at all knows that if they are very ill, the visit of a sensitive priest or trained lay person (who are more and more sharing in this work) saying at the bedside some strong and familiar prayer, really does help. It literally does take us into another dimension. So, St Christopher's, like some other Hospices, has at its heart the chapel, the daily Eucharist and prayers, and the ministry of all the Christian doctors, nurses and auxiliaries – not pressing religion on people, but enabling those with a faith to die with their hope strengthened and those without faith to keep the door of hope open. For, when all is said and done, there is an inescapable sadness in death. This sadness needs to be set within the context of a greater gain and a fuller vision. One of the greatest thinkers of all times was St Thomas Aquinas. The starting point for Aquinas was that we are all searching for happiness – and I don't think anyone would disagree with that. He explores all the different kinds of happiness and concludes that we cannot find final or lasting happiness in anything created. 'The object of the will, that is the human appetite,' he writes, 'is the Good without reserve, just as the object of the mind is the True without reserve.' Clearly then, nothing can satisfy man's will except such goodness, which is found, not in anything created, but in God alone. 'There can be no complete and final happiness for us', he writes, 'save in the

vision of God'. A difficult thought – but one
which can illuminate our earthly parting.

O God, from you we come
and to you, at the last, we return.
Be with us now and in the hour of our death.

Through The Christian Year

Advent

Advent is, I think, my favourite part of the church's year: which is odd. For the traditional themes of Advent, death, judgement, heaven and hell hardly fill us with delight. So why, despite this, is Advent such a lovely time? First, it has to be said, even though it may not be a fair point, Advent has some superb hymns and music. I'm not a great hymn singer myself, and indeed would on the whole do without them altogether. But the music of Advent has a really thrilling quality to it.

Then, secondly, Advent is a time of spare beauty. It perfectly matches nature at this season. The trees are stripped of their leaves and they stand there, silhouetted against the winter sky, austere of line, mysterious and haunting. Advent reflects this. It is a time for being stripped down to essentials. There is a proper place in life for overdoing it, we call it feasting. But fasting, or getting ready, has, in its own way, an even greater attraction. Lent of course is also a time of preparation but it's got all so mixed up with odd and grim ideas. Advent is an attractive time and it reminds us of the beauty of simplicity. It is a time for getting back to the fundamentals of life and this simplicity, this poverty before God, has, like the trees, a spare and haunting beauty.

Then, finally, of course, Advent is a time of expectation, of hope – and how much we need hope at the moment. The Church's hope in this season is a rich, multi-layered concept. It is hope for the coming of the Lord in glory, when all that is wrong in the world will be made right. And it is hope for the coming of the Lord in humility when our hard hearts will melt before the sun. Both these expressions of hope are rooted in the Old Testament. One of the priceless gifts which the Jewish people have given to the world is this hope. It all goes back to them. Hope is a constant theme in their history – in the wilderness, during the captivity in Babylon in the fifth century BC – when they were under Greek and Roman rule. And that's another thing that's nice about Advent – those excellent readings from the Old Testament, particularly the book of Isaiah. For it is there that the hopes of the world have their origin including, as a matter of fact, the Marxist hope of a better world. Human hopes have so often been dashed to the ground or twisted. Human beings are continuously disillusioned. It is tempting to say with the French writer, Camus: 'Let us think clearly and not hope any more'. Yet hope, like cheerfulness, keeps breaking in. This hope is no illusion. For there *is* something to look forward to; and for this future, God's future, we were made.

Lord, you come in glory at the end of time.
You come in humility at Christmas.
Come today in the secret places of our heart.

Christmas

A colleague said to me once 'I hate Christmas. I don't know how I'm going to get through it.' He's not a difficult person. On the contrary, nice and rather intelligent. So it's possible there are other nice and rather intelligent people who would admit to a fellow feeling. I suppose our patron Saint, if I can speak of our, is Scrooge.

'A merry Christmas, uncle! God save you!' cried a cheerful voice. It was the voice of Scrooge's nephew, who came upon him so quickly that this was the first intimation he had of his appearance.

'Bah!' said Scrooge, 'Humbug!'

Later some carol singers 'stooped down at Scrooge's keyhole to regale him with a Christmas carol; but at the first sound of

'God rest you merry gentlemen,
May nothing you dismay,'

Scrooge seized the ruler with such energy of action, that the singer fled in terror, leaving the keyhole to the fog and even more congenial frost.'

Rather extreme behaviour; but it being Christmas, a time for goodwill, perhaps we ought to try to understand Scrooge. Could it be that he was really a person of very strong emotions? That Christmas moved him deeply? And like other people of strong emotion he could not cope with them, did not dare show them even to himself? And the nearer Christmas came with its air of generosity and joie de vivre, the more threatening it all came to poor Scrooge who had to batten down his feelings more tightly by displaying ever more tightness and irritation?

Scrooge has become a byword for all that is ungenerous; the archetypal anti-hero. Yet I suppose that Dickens would not have succeeded in creating a character of such universal infamy unless he had projected what is in all of us. After all, those characters who spilled out onto the pages of Dickens actually came from inside him; and if they came from inside him and engage us, they are there somewhere inside us as well.

In the story by Dickens, Scrooge eventually breaks. 'Heaven and Christmastime be praised for this!' he says, 'I say it on my knees, on my knees.' The Christmas atmosphere, the Christian love of the Scratchitt family and his wrestling with some mysterious supernatural spirit broke through to him and released his pent-up feelings of generosity and happiness. 'I don't know what to do', cried Scrooge, laughing and crying in the same breath, 'I am as light as a feather, I am as happy as an angel'. Now I can well understand if that all seems a bit too much! But what *A Christmas Carol* describes is what God is doing all the time, taking the initiative towards us, breaking down the tight, grumpy, niggardly front we use to keep the world at bay, letting our pent-up feelings of generosity and affirmation peep out. The Old Testament is a story of heaven reaching out to earth; in Christ heavenly hands are held out to their furthest point. The eternal Son of God comes amongst us as a human being. What happened uniquely then is a sign of what God does, in a million different ways, all the time.

May God bless us
and though we can't all be cheerful – certainly not all of the time –
may he give us that deeper joy that comes from life in Christ.

New Year

'Marriage has many pains, but celibacy has no pleasures.' Dr. Johnson of course. 'Politics are now nothing more than a means of rising in the world.' Dr. Johnson again, one of the most quoted men in the English language. Always trenchant, funny, full of common sense. Yet, for all his humour, Johnson was a man who, all his life, struggled against depression: Which is perhaps why the playwright Samuel Beckett, so different in belief, is drawn towards him. And therefore it is not surprising that for Samuel Johnson, and for so many people, New Year's Eve was a bad time. He looked back on the past year, and despite the fact that he was a man of prodigious energy, he wondered what, if anything, he had really achieved. He looked at the year ahead full of fear and foreboding. He wondered what the year would bring; wondered whether it would be his last.

We know what Dr. Johnson felt about the New Year because on January 1st 1745 and on almost every New Year's day thereafter, he composed a prayer for himself. From the notes that he left we can gather that he probably did this in the small hours of the morning. These prayers begin with a sense of surprise - indeed gratitude, that he had survived another year. 'Almighty God by whose mercy I am permitted to behold the beginning of another year.' Johnson then went on to express his anxieties, 'Mitigate, if it shall seem best unto thee, the diseases of my body, and compose the disorders of my mind. Dispel my terrors.' As he got older his prayers reflect an awareness of the difficulties and temptations of old age. 'As age comes upon me', he wrote in one prayer, 'let my mind be more withdrawn from vanity and folly.'

And in another, 'Let not the cares of the world distract me, nor the evils of age overwhelm me.' Finally, as he contemplated the life that might be left to him and the work he might get done during that time, he prayed, 'Let me perform to thy glory and the good of my fellow creatures the work which thou shalt yet appoint me.'

The beginning of the New Year is a strange time; a time full of poignancy; a time of regrets, of hopes, of anxieties; a time of feelings that we do not dare, and hardly know how, to put into words; a time when we are deeply conscious of the mystery, the sadness and the courage of human existence. Almost every year, about 2am in the morning, Dr. Johnson put these feelings of his in a prayer. Although by nature he was a remarkably speedy writer, rarely correcting his work, he intimated he took two or three hours over these little prayers. Perhaps we might say, 'We are what we pray' – when, after a real struggle for the right words, we pray.

Of course we may be jumping in the water in Trafalgar Square, or lifting a glass of wine round at a friend's house, or holding hands with others singing Auld Lang Syne. All this too is part of life, but underneath – and on our own – there is the other side of the mystery. It helps sometimes to put it into words, perhaps as Dr. Johnson did, into the words of a prayer.

Epiphany

Epiphany in the early days of the church was much more important than Christmas. In the west the feast is associated above all with the visit of those three mysterious strangers to the Christ child. Who were they? What were they like? The story has both haunted and fired the imagination of people in every age. By the fifth century the three magi had become three kings; by the eight century they had got names; and by the fourteenth Kaspar had become a Moor. The story has inspired innumerable painters. Christmas cards often show reproductions of some of the many famous paintings depicting the Kings in all their finery kneeling down before the Christ child. In our own time the story has inspired novelists and poets. In this story, perhaps more than any other, we are conscious of the unity of religion and culture in our heritage and of what a rich treasury of painting, music and poetry it is.

But what did Matthew himself mean by the story? One of the insights of modern biblical scholarship is that the writers of the Gospels weren't dull chaps just copying out legal documents. They were artists in their own right. They had a point of view, a story to tell. And Matthew gives us two clues to what he meant. First, you remember there is a famous story in the Old Testament about the visit of the Queen of Sheba to King Solomon with her tribute of gold and spices. Well, a commentary on that story mentions that she was guided by a star. The second clue is provided by another passage in Matthew, chapter 12, verse 42, where Jesus says to his followers: 'The Queen of the South will arise at the judgement with this generation and condemn it; for she came from the ends of the earth to hear the wisdom of Solomon, and behold, something greater than Solomon is here.' *Something greater than Soloman is here.* That is what Matthew wanted to say in this story. As the Queen of Sheba came from the South, guided by a star, so now three sages come, also guided by a star, to worship before the Christ child; one greater than Solomon even from his birth, the King of Kings. That's how Matthew interpreted the event. What should we make of it?

Here is the last part of the story in the AV:

And lo, the star, which they saw in the east, went before them, till it came and stood over where the young child was.
When they saw the star, they rejoiced with exceeding great joy.
And when they were come into the house, they saw the young child with Mary his mother, and fell down, and worshipped him: and when they had opened their treasures, they presented unto him gifts; gold, and frankincense and myrrh.

O God, who by the leading of a star didst manifest thy only begotten Son to the Gentiles; Mercifully grant, that we, which know thee now by faith, may after this life have the fruition of thy glorious Godhead; through Jesus Christ our Lord.

How Should We Use Lent?

When St Thomas More died, a hair shirt was found next to his skin. This great man, scholar, wit, friend and Chancellor of England kept himself in permanent discomfort in order always to remind himself of the fundamental realities of life. Wearing hair shirts has gone out of fashion – I'm glad to say. But what disciplines, if any, are appropriate today?

We all live our lives according to a series of rhythms, sleeping and waking, work and play, night and day. The church offers us another rhythm which I find both helpful and healthy: fast and feast, denial and celebration. Some people scowl even at the thought of keeping Christmas Day, but for those who are caught up in the cycle of the Church's year, Advent, Christmas, Epiphany, Lent, Easter, Whitsun, Trinity and so on, it is a source of continuous delight. It suffuses the natural order, Autumn, Winter, Spring, and Summer, with a supernatural charm and steadiness. Lent is one of the preludes to feast and celebration. It is a time for getting back to essentials. And as bare trees in winter have an austere beauty no less miraculous than when they are in full leaf, so Lent can have its own spare delight.

But how should we use Lent? Here are two general principles. First, to look at the minimum expectations we have of ourselves as human beings. Sometimes we have slipped even below our own minimum, sometimes we realise that minimum is so low we would like to raise it a notch. And is it unfair to suggest that the national minimum for religion is most extraordinarily low? The Poles bring it home to us, don't they? For they think nothing of going into Mass every morning on the way to work. It was brought home to me in South Africa in the large black African township of Soweto. In one Anglican parish everyone belonged to a house group which would meet three times a week for an hour's prayer and planning, deciding which acts of neighbourliness they would carry out in the next day or so. In an essay he wrote in 1938, T.S.Eliot wrote, 'The Anglo-Saxons display a capacity for diluting their religion probably in excess of that of every other race.' I don't think things have changed much since then.

Secondly, to reflect on what in our best moments we ask of ourselves. Someone once defined faith as 'Life lived on the evidence of its highest moments.' If this is so, then discipline comes in not as self-punishment but as a way of underpinning or undergirding our lives between those better moments, which are sometimes very far apart. In our better moments we are sometimes full of good intentions. What matters is that these send us to the tool-box to get out some suitable nuts and bolts to underpin our lives, ie certain specific, practical, manageable things we can do and firmly resolve to do.

O Lord, who for our sake didst fast forty days and forty nights: give us grace to use such abstinence, that, our flesh being subdued to the spirit, we may ever obey they godly motions in righteousness and true holiness, to thy honour and glory: who livest and reignest with the Father and the Holy Spirit, one God, world without end.

Good Friday

Patrick White's important novel *The Riders in the Chariot* is set in Australia. It's about four strange, isolated people: old Miss Hare who lives in a tumbledown mansion; Alf Dubbo, a half aboriginee derelict; Mrs Goldbold, a saintly cleaning lady; and Himmelfarb, a German Jew who managed to escape the Nazi death chamber. What these four characters have in common is a spiritual view of life which they experience in terms of the vision of the fiery chariot in the book of Ezekiel. Each of the four is a rider in this Divine chariot. The climax of the novel comes on Good Friday: and that year this coincides with passover which Himmelfarb is preparing to celebrate. But, before doing so, he goes into the factory where he works. And there, in a frightening scene, he is forced to undergo a mock crucifixion. All the hurt and desire to hurt, and all the latent anti-semitism in his jokey workmates comes to the surface. They string Himmelfarb up on a tree. All the ingredients are there, bashing, blood, and the crowd of onlookers taunting and jeering. A very ugly and unpleasant scene. But it is clearly Patrick White's purpose to suggest that the same evil forces which were at work in Nazi Germany are at work in Australian suburbia. And this has provoked some very interesting reactions from literary critics. One, for example, has written that the book does

not work because societies just do differ qualita-
tively, 'the hell of Auschwitz and Buchenwald' he
writes 'is not the hell of Australian suburbia . . .'
Another critic however disagrees and suggests
that White is not concerned 'with the relative
merits of two societies but with the indissoluble
connection of forms of human evil. Each, whether
extreme or near, comes from the corrupt will or
the clouded understanding.'

This is not a mere academic exercise but a
question that has to be discussed in relation to
every human society, including our own. Could
Auschwitz or its equivalent happen here? Or do
societies really differ? In one way they do. I like to
think that there is a certain tolerance and balance
and civilisation that has been built into the texture
of our national life that would, even in an extreme
situation, stop us from killing millions of people
we don't like. However, the second critic is also
right. There is an indissoluble connection between
different forms of evil. My negligence, weakness
and deliberate wrong doing is not different in kind
from the negligence, weakness and deliberate
wrong doing of other people in other ages, which
has been responsible for the terrible toll of human
history; and whose starkest revelation is in the fact
that we crucified God himself. It's not a nice
thought but Good Friday expresses one terrible,
inescapable aspect of the truth about mankind.
But it's not the only aspect. The other is the hope
that arises out of the Christian conviction that it is
God himself who was in that lonely, battered figure
on the cross. This was not just one more wretched
sufferer. In that pain and darkness Jesus Chist

allowed himself to suffer the consequences of our sin and folly; he died the death of a blasphemer, of one who was accursed. But because of his unbroken unity with his father through it all he broke the power of evil. For the resurrection reveals this to be a triumph over hell, and this blasphemer to be most blessed.

Almighty God, we beseech thee graciously to behold this thy family, for which our Lord Jesus Christ was contented to be betrayed, and given up into the hands of wicked men, and to suffer death upon the cross, who now liveth and reigneth with thee and the Holy Ghost, ever one God, world without end.

Amen.

The Risen Christ

Oscar Wilde has a high reputation as a writer of comedies. His plays are still staged and *The Importance of Being Ernest* must have brought laughter to millions. But people remember Oscar Wilde as much for his life as his plays. He had an extravagant, often outrageous personality. He didn't fit easily into conventional society which was often shocked by what he said and did. In 1895 he was jailed for two years. Whilst in prison he wrote a long letter which contained these words about Christ. 'By being brought into his presence one becomes something. And everybody is predestined to his presence. Once at least in his life each man walks with Christ to Emmaus.' Emmaus you remember was the village near Jerusalem to which two disciples were walking shortly after the death of Christ when a stranger joined them. On the journey they talked together about recent happenings and at the end, as they blessed and broke bread together, the disciples recognised that the stranger was none other than Christ himself who at once vanished from their sight. I wonder what it was in his own experience that made Oscar Wilde say that at least once in his life, each man walks with Christ to Emmaus?

Oscar Wilde loathed prison. He wrote. 'I have lain in prison for nearly two years. Out of my nature has come wild despair; and abandonment to grief that was piteous to look at; terrible and impotent rage; bitterness and scorn; anguish that wept aloud.' Yet during this time he learnt the value of sorrow. He wrote 'Behind joy and laughter there may be a temperament coarse, hard and callous. But behind sorrow there is always sorrow. Pain, unlike pleasure, wears no mask.' He believed that this sorrow had enabled him to perceive things he had never seen before; that it gave him a more truthful perspective on life. In particular it brought him to discover in himself what he called humility but which is perhaps better described as acceptance of life without resentment or bitterness. 'I am completely penniless, and absolutely homeless', he wrote 'Yet there are worse things in the world than that. I am quite candid when I say that rather than go out of this prison with bitterness in my heart against the world, I would gladly and readily beg my bread from door to door.'

This new way of approaching life, what he called his new life, was related to his continuing reflection on the person of Christ. He wrote that 'Every morning after I have cleaned my cell and polished my tins, I read a little of the gospels . . . It is a delightful way of opening the day. Everyone, even in a turbulent, ill-disciplined life, should do the same.'

Oscar Wilde wasn't a naturally religious person. At one point he wrote 'Religion doesn't help me. The faith that others give to what is unseen, I give to what one can touch and look at . . . I feel I would like to found an order for those who *cannot* believe.' Yet in prison, reflecting on his own

94

experience and the person in the Gospels, he discovered what he felt was a new, more truthful attitude to life. Before he died he was received into the church. In his pain and humiliation he had walked with a stranger whom later he came to see was Christ. I don't think he had what we would call a mystical experience. Rather it was a question of thinking hard about the meaning of his life and what had happened to him, in the light of the Gospels. He found that his own dawning insights were both confirmed and deepened by the Gospel truths.

O God grant that as we reflect on the experiences that happen to us your truth and your presence may illuminate our sorrows and our joys.

O Holy Spirit – Fill Me

Lilian Baylis was a legendary figure in the theatre. She started by helping her aunt run a temperance hall. When her aunt died in 1912 she devoted herself to turning it into a fulfilment of her own ideals, a theatre where opera and drama could be brought to everyone. It became the Old Vic. Later she opened Sadler's Wells. Sir John Gielgud has written of her that she had 'this extraordinary belief that she was there for a purpose which it was her duty to carry out'. She was obviously a formidable lady and sometimes she treated God with the same forthrightness that others experienced. 'O God send me actors and make them cheap' is one prayer she is reputed to have said.

When Lilian Baylis died there was found amongst her belongings a list of people for whom she prayed each day and a favourite prayer written out in her own handwriting, a lovely prayer to the Holy Spirit. The prayer has one particularly striking thought. 'I offer thee the one thing I really possess, my capacity for being filled with thee.' Whether we live in the country or in the tough world of theatre or commerce, we are an emptiness that longs to be filled. This emptiness is not a negative thing, it is a capacity. We sometimes read on a drum 'capacity 10 gallons'. Capacities are there to be filled. Without the Holy Spirit we are nothing. It is only through the Holy Spirit, God within us, that we come to believe at all. It is only through the Holy Spirit that we can pray at all; for true prayer is always the Holy Spirit praying in and through us. It is only through the Holy Spirit that we are capable of any genuine good, for only that which is of God within us is good. Without the Holy Spirit we are an emptiness. But this emptiness is a capacity waiting to be filled. This was the prayer found amonst Lilian Baylis's things. It was written by W.J.Carey, who was Bishop of Blomfontein from 1921–1934 and founder of the Village Evengelists. He recommended that it be said slowly; or brooded over; or thought and felt.

O Holy Spirit of God –
come into my heart and fill me:
I open the windows of my soul to let thee in.
I surrender my whole life to thee:
come and possess me, fill me with light and
    truth.
I offer to thee the one thing I really possess,
my capacity for being filled by thee.
Of myself I am an unprofitable servant,
an empty vessel.
Fill me so that I may live the life of the Spirit:
The life of truth and goodness, the life of beauty
    and love,
the life of wisdom and strength.
And guide me today in all things:
guide me to the people I should meet or help:
to the circumstances in which I can best serve
    thee,

whether by my action, or by my sufferings.
But, above all, make Christ to be formed in me,
that I may dethrone self in my heart
and make him king.
Bind and cement me to Christ by all thy ways
known and unknown:
by Holy thoughts, and unseen graces,
and sacramental ties:
so that he is in me, and I in him,
today, and for ever.

Transfiguration

Glory is not a word that our generation is very keen on. I suspect it was an idea that went out with the guns and carnage of the First World War. Yet the church cannot quite give up the notion and it is intimately associated with the Feast of the Transfiguration, one of the great days in the Christian year. The close friends of Jesus were with him on a mountain when he was transfigured before them and they beheld his glory. Then there is that marvellous line from St Paul, 'And we, beholding the glory of the Lord, are being changed into his likeness, from one degree of glory to another.' Glory, on the Christian view of things, is an ultimate constituent of the Universe. It shows through in Christ: but it belongs to God in origin and to us by association.

What meaning, however, can we give to the word? My starting point is that we all live for something. Most often we live for ourselves. We find it hard if others don't notice us. We want the world to like us, be pleased with us, praise us, even if only in our own circle. At its extreme, we may say about someone – he's only interested in his own glory. But at other times we live for something other than ourselves. I think of a person whose whole life has been in the service of his county cricket club, first as player, then as secretary, then on the committee. 'He lives for cricket', we say. People do live for the glory of something else; club, school, institution or country. Yet in the end can anything finite hold us? Some lines have become part of our heritage, first of all adopted by the Jesuits as their motto – Ad Majorem Dei Gloriam – to the greater Glory of God. The great Johann Sebastian Bach, a Lutheran, used to put the initials of this motto at the bottom of his scores, AMDG. He wanted his music to glorify God, not himself.

At the memorial service for Eric Abbott, a predecessor of mine, Westminster Abbey was packed. 'What had he got?' asked someone who did not know him. A good question, for though able, he was no cleverer than thousands of others. He had the gift of friendship, yet I doubt that that alone would have brought nearly 2,000 to the Abbey. In the service, there was an extract from one of his own writings. I suspect that people sensed in Eric Abott himself the truth of those words he once wrote:

'*Ad Majorem Dei Gloriam*' This will afford us the same motive as Christ our Lord had. This will direct all our work to an end beyond ourselves. This will afford us a worthy ambition – the glory of God and the kingdom of God. It will also lift us out of our self-centredness, to look beyond our own glory to God's. It will give us a simple and salutary form of self-examination, "*Whose* is the glory I am seeking, in the things I do and say?"'

Lord of Glory
Help us to live
not for ourselves
but for the glory of the Father.

God In Life

Work

Sometimes strikes make it difficult to get to work. But most people still struggle in somehow. One of my younger colleagues said that he was amazed at the resolve people show. He and his wife, he suggested, would never go to such lengths to get to work. Was it, he wondered, because he was a welfare state baby, brought up soft? But it can't be that. For a high percentage of those who drive through the small hours and wait for hours in bus queues or traffic jams, are also welfare state babies. What is it about work that draws us so? Philip Larkin begins one of his poems:

What should I let the toad *work*
Squat on my life?
Can't I use my wit as pitchfork
And drive the brute off?

Six days of the week it soils
With its sickening poison –
Just for paying a few bills!
That's out of proportion.

But he concludes that he is incapable of getting rid of the toad or of shouting:

'Stuff your pension'

For something sufficiently toad-like
Squats in me, too.

A later collection returns to the same them. A
Poem called 'Toads Revisited' begins:

Walking around in the park
Should feel better than work:
The lake, the sunshine,
The grass to lie on

but when he sees the other people in the park
he is glad he has a job:

No, give me my in-tray,
My loaf-haired secretary,
My shall-I-keep-the-call-in-Sir:

Give me your arm, old toad;
Help me down Cemetery Road.

Larkin is right in discerning some strange,
somewhat depressing reasons why we work. But
there are of course more positive ones, not least
the sheer necessity for most of us of actually
earning a living. Then there are people who
genuinely enjoy their work, or the people they
meet there, or they value having an acknowledged
place in the community, something which the
retired and the unemployed often badly miss. So
there are a variety of motives present. Let me
focus on just one. Work is not only a way or
earning a living; not just a means to personal
fulfilment. It can also be an offering, our contribu-

tion to the community. We are all dependent on others, every moment of every day we receive what they have given. Work, whether it is paid employment or things we do in a voluntary capacity, is part of our response. For the person of faith it can also be part of our response to God. There are some marvellous words of St Paul:

Therefore, my beloved brethren, be ye steadfast, unmoveable, always abounding in the work of the Lord, forasmuch as ye know that your labour is not in vain in the Lord.

Whatever the funny old mixture of motives that take us to work, that work can also be seen as an offering; an offering to the community and through the community to God. Such labour is not in vain.

Heavenly Father, I lift to you the work of this day: an offering of love for others, an offering of love for you. Make my work an extension of your work in the world.

Law and Liberty

I imagine everyone who watches mass picketing on TV finds it unpleasant. Neverthless, even when such scenes are put before us I think we should thank God for the possibility of strikes. For they are a sign that our society is still free. Strikes are ugly boils on the skin but the blood of liberty, though poisoned, still flows in our veins: Which it doesn't in so many other countries. If we value our fundamental freedoms, freedom of speech, freedom of association, freedom of the press, we have to accept the inevitability of conflict. As Professor Dahrendorf has said: 'Conflict is liberty, because by conflict alone the multitude and incompatibility of human interests and desires find adequate expression in a world of notorious uncertainty.' Furthermore, liberty can only exist where people have enough power to make their voice heard, to get themselves taken seriously. Which, of course, is why union legislation is always contentious. It is about power, who has it and how much. Every generation has to strike the balance anew. Whether the present Government has got it right or wrong is not my present concern, which is the general point well expressed by Thomas Hobbs: 'Liberty', he said, 'is power cut into pieces'; and liberty is a fundamental Christian value.

Freedom means different things to different

people. Within this country it means freedom within a framework of law. Law, of course, is never entirely neutral. The unions often feel now, as they have felt in the past, that legislation is biased against them. The Government feels it expresses the bias of society as a whole. But though law is never totally neutral true law is, from a Christian point of view, an attempt to relate human ordering to the divine law. At one time in this country there was a majestic vision of law in the scheme of things; it was a grand design built like one of the great Cathedrals. We tend to think of law as something negative and restrictive. It's what stops you parking your car where you want when you are in a hurry. But according to St Thomas Aquinas, law is 'an ordinance of reason for the common good'. In other words, it is something reasonable that exists for our benefit and it begins not with us but with the mind of God. For there is, according to him, an eternal law – God's guidance for our happiness – and all human law is related to this. First of all, natural law – those basic moral values which all reason-able human beings can assent to, whatever their religious beliefs, and then our human laws, which must be grounded in this natural law. What a grand, architectonic scheme it was: the eternal law designed to guide us into the way of happiness, natural laws that we can discover by using our minds – and human laws which we must strive to make just and which we must obey, because they are ultimately grounded in the Eternal law. It is a vision which our society as a whole, not just a few people, has lost.

Grant O God
in all the conflict of our society
as we strive to balance power with power
and order our affairs for the common good,
we may be inspired by a new vision of
your mind and your law.

Mercy in Prison and Mercy on us All

I once spent a day in Wakefield with the chaplains to our toughest prisons. I don't know if it was any use to them but it was certainly good for me to have to think about a subject that I suspect most of us are inclined to push out of sight.

What is the purpose of prisons? One chaplain said that over the last decade the whole understanding of what prisons are for has undergone a radical change. One of the prime purposes used to be the rehabilitation of the prisoner so that he could take his place in society as a law-abiding citizen. Now, I was told, prisons are seen mainly as places of custody where prisoners have the choice, if they so wish, to enrich their life through education or religion, but without any pressure to do so. There was a feeling amongst the chaplains that in this new emphasis there was some loss but also one big gain. This philosophy showed more respect for the dignity of prisoners. They were not objects to be manipulated, even with the best intentions. It was up to them, as it is up to us, to choose.

It was also good for me to realise that there are many Christians in prison – probably a higher percentage there than in the population as a whole. It is so easy to equate Christianity with respectability. But, as William Blake put it:

'If moral virtue was Christianity, Christ's pretensions were all vanity'.

Of course there are some Christian success stories. There have been convicted murderers, who have been converted in prison, and who have then served the church. But there are also Christian failures, in prison as elsewhere. I was told about someone, fairly typical, who went to church in prison and made a real effort, but when out slipped back somewhat until he came in again and tried to pick himself up once more. Sad of course – but are we really able to judge the extent of people's successes and failures? When Randolph Churchill and Evelyn Waugh were together in Yugoslavia in the war they did not get on at all. After one particularly violent quarrel Randolph Churchill shouted out, 'And I thought you were meant to be a Christian and a Catholic', to which Waugh replied, 'And think how much worse I would be if I wasn't'.

Prison chaplains seem to me to be a most powerful symbol. On the one hand they are citizens like anyone else, and therefore responsible with the rest of us for locking up thousands of people every year for the protection of society. They are also priests and ministers of the Gospel, coming in from the outside to offer God's forgiveness. And at the same time they themselves stand not one whit less in need of God's forgiveness and grace than the most hardened criminal. That, as I understand it, is their situation – not so very different from ours.

Heavenly Father,
We hold in your presence all prisoners
and those working in the Prison Service.
In the midst of so much sadness and tragedy
May we know your mercy and discover
fresh hope.

Poverty

In Brecht's famous play Galileo says, 'Virtues don't depend on misery, my friend. If your family were well off and happy, they'd have all the virtues being well off and happy brings. These virtues of exhausted men come from exhausted fields and I reject them.' I like this for the way it strips the romantic gloss off poverty. Poverty brings drudgery, disease, suffering and degradation. There are people in the world, 600 million of them, who suffer from malnutrition; people in Britain who live below the state defined poverty line – 5 million of them, and that's not the whole story. These are all people like ourselves. In our time the solutions are, inescapably, political – exactly what they are is open to debate, but that there must be solutions, is the concern of us all.

There I wish I could leave it – for Christianity seems to confuse the issue. 'Blessed are the poor', said Jesus. 'Blessed are the poor, for theirs is the kingdom of heaven'. How can this be? Colin Winter, the former Bishop of Namibia, spoke once on why we loved the poor. 'They are my friends and liberators', he said, 'for they show me that God reigns, that his love shines out in shanties, in prisons and in dark hovels and that darkness does not overcome it. He has allowed me to see Him, bleeding, broken, despised and rejected, but undeterred and unconquered in the faces of the struggling, hope-filled poor.' The poor are blessed because sometimes their poverty, instead of degrading them, brings out their dignity, brings them to share what little they have with others, leads them to concentrate with joy on essentials, forces them, through their nothingness, to rely on and reveal the everythingness of God. There seems to me no way of getting round the message of Jesus that the true church belongs to the poor. The blessing in the Roman Catholic marriage service gets it right. The priest says to the kneeling couple, 'May you always bear witness to the love of God in this world so that the afflicted and the needy will find in you generous friends and welcome you into the joys of heaven.'

All this is troubling. A tramp once told me about what happened when he asked a minister for money. 'Pray to the Lord', he was told, 'and he will give it to you.' 'I tell you what', replied the tramp, 'you give me what you've got and then you pray to the Lord. He's more likely to hear you than me'. The sad fact is we clutch and cling to what we've got; we are reluctant to let go, reluctant to share. And the more we have, the stronger the tendency is likely to be. 'It is easier for a camel to go through the eye of a needle than for a rich man to enter the kingdom of God'. Perhaps the way to begin to unprise this tenacious clinging is to bring to mind the time in our lives when we certainly join the poor. 'We brought nothing into this world', said Job, 'and it is certain we can carry nothing out'. At the end we all join the poor. The supremely difficult, supremely worthwhile task, is to join them before.

Lord Jesus Christ,
Eternal Son of God,
Born in a stable,
Son of Man with nowhere to lay your head.
Bring quickly the time when
Your brothers born on the earth
May grow up free from want and fear,
And grant that we all may join
Those poor whom you promised to be blessed.

Those Who Wait

All of us spend much time waiting: waiting for a bus, waiting in a traffic jam, waiting to be served. Some people spend nearly all day waiting, the housebound for example; waiting for the lady from meals on wheels or the promised telephone call in the evening. Society conditions us to think of waiting as a waste of time, something to be hurried through as quickly as possible. This is serious, because the older we get the less active we are likely to become; and the more time we will spend simply waiting. So let me, if I may, point to two aspects of waiting that reveal its value. First, if we are waiting for someone, it means that person matters to us. A parent lying awake at night waiting for a child to come in from a party; or a child waiting for a parent to come in from work. A state of mind where nothing mattered to us, where we were totally indifferent to everything would be worrying. The fact that we are waiting for something, however small, is a sign of our humanity; of our capacity to be affected by experience.

Secondly, when we are forced to wait we often notice what would otherwise pass us by. Waiting at the station I become aware of the austere beauty of bare branches against a winter sky. So familiar, yet so haunting. This kind of noticing is not just a camera-like recording. What we see is significant for us. Perhaps that's why people who are confined to bed or hospital for long periods come to be affected strongly by a kind word or a harsh one; by tasty food, or indifferent cooking. Their focus is narrowed and they are forced to feel the significance of everything, however small.

These two reasons suggest that our capacity to wait is a sign of our capacity to love, our capacity to be affected by the universe, our capacity to see its meaning and significance. And in an excellent book *The Stature of Waiting*, W.H. Vanstone shows how this is rooted in God himself. God is creator, yes; and through our activity we share in his work. But God also waits. Like a creative artist he waits upon the outcome of his work, which in the case of the earth includes our free choices and responses. God waits, and is affected by, his creatures. He receives as well as initiates. And we can become co-receivers with him, as well as co-creators. There is a stature, a human and a divine dignity in waiting, no less than in activity. And in our time, with an increasingly large proportion of the population over 60, and with over three million not in paid jobs, this is a kind of dignity we desperately need to recover. So, as Vanstone puts it, 'God creates a world which includes among its infinite variety of wonders this culminating wonder – that there are points within it at which, in the consciousness of men, its wonders are received and recognised.'

Heavenly Father,
Bless those constricted by circumstances,
All those forced to wait,
Especially those confined to home or bed.
Help them, and us,
To grow in awareness.

Cancer

John Robinson, the former Bishop of Woolwich, died in December 1983. You may remember him as the author of *Honest to God*; not, in my judgement, a book which will stand up to dispassionate, philosophical analysis, but a book which did help literally millions to locate God in their lives. John Robinson directed people to look within themselves, at their own deepest convictions. There, he said, in that stirring and longing and commitment, you will discover the divine touching your soul. He helped people in their spiritual quest and so it is above all as a pastor that I like to think of him: and in nothing was he more of a pastor than in his dying.

Preaching two years ago at the funeral of a girl of 16 who had died of cancer, John Robinson said that 'God was to be found in the cancer as much as in the sunset'. As he himself was dying of cancer he told people how that statement had come true for him. It did not mean, he stressed, that God sends cancer to test or try us: such a God would be intolerable. So what did he mean? First, it set him thinking about the cause of cancer. He didn't know the cause but he did know that hidden resentments and unresolved conflicts within us sometimes make their presence felt through physical illness. His cancer made him look at what he called his unfinished agenda and to face, come to terms with – and a stronger word than that – embrace, things about himself he had tended to hide away. This is the spirit of God, who searches us out and knows us, leading us into the truth about ourselves and a true love of ourselves.

Secondly, he became aware of the many people who cared for him. No doubt, he said, it was all there before, but as a result of the cancer he had become aware through the giving and receiving in his relationships with his family and friends, of grace upon grace. Thirdly, when he was given only a few months to live he re-examined his priorities and decided to do only what really mattered. He went on holiday with his wife, he finished off some scholarly work and above all he tried to make his life really life; life with a capital L and not mere existence. This life, which the New Testament calls 'Eternal Life' 'is begun, continued but not ended now', he said. It is not ended with death but it has to begin and develop now.

In these three ways John Robinson said he had found God in his cancer as much as in the sunset. We get lost if we try to work out why horrible things happen to some people and not others. Star golfer, Ballesteros, a deeply religious man, was due to travel in a plane in which all lives were lost, but switched tickets at the last moment. He blesses God, but we wonder about the person who got his ticket at the last moment. On those intellectual questions we have no answer. Where we do have an answer is in our living and dying. In every situation we can find God and co-operate with him in bringing forth some unique good from our pain and muddle and tragedy.

Lord,
You are to be found in all the experiences of the
    day,
Grant us to seek you, find you
and join with you.
For in all things you are working for good
with those who love you.

'For Christ's Sake' – in South Africa

I once visited South Africa, where I was invited to give a series of talks. Like most people I was interested to find out whether things had really got better; and on the face of it, they have. In the international hotels and in some big international organisations people of all races are accepted on more equal terms than in the past. So if you go as a tourist or on a quick business trip you will probably get the impression that things are improving. But underneath, I'm afraid, apartheid is as ugly, vicious and ruthless as it ever was and new legislation is making it even worse. I saw terrible poverty, I heard accounts of intimidation and brutality. Yet these are but the painful symptons of the killer disease itself. The disease, linked to the so called homelands policy, is systematically depriving millions of people of all the basic rights of citizenship that you and I take for granted. As one of the architects of the plan, Dr. Connie Hulder, said 'Soon there will be no black South Africans.' 20 million people, 86% of the population, are being given 5% of the land, the most arid land, and being made foreigners in the country of their birth – except of course where, with special permits, they are allowed to reside temporarily as migrant workers. However sincerely conceived, it is a wicked system. I was shocked by very many things but distressed as much as anything else by the continuous tide of propoganda, and the slanting of the news, the disinformation which keeps so many in the white community in apparent ignorance of the true state of the country and the growing resentment under the laughter and patience of the majority.

Yet that was not all I experienced. I also encountered some most marvellous people. For a variety of reasons, some good, some bad, South Africa is a deeply religious country in a way that we have not been since the 17th century. In this country politics and religion tend to inhabit different worlds. On the one hand we have the rasping, cliché ridden, language of politics. On the other hand we have a religion that has become cosy and privatised. In South Africa where the issues are so stark, and where every aspect of life has a political dimension, religious commitment and political commitment tend to fuse together. I had the privilege of speaking to a wide range of people, many of them very well known, including Bishop Desmond Tutu, and Helen Joseph, both of whom I am proud to say are former students, and Fellows, of King's College, London. But what remains in my mind as much as anything else is a simple remark by a young black priest as he drove me through the dust of Soweto to meet members of his congregation. He said about some political issue 'I must make a stand for Christ's sake.' The sentence rang absolutely true. The phrase 'for Christ's sake' was no pious gloss. His struggle, like that of so many black Christians, even now, is rooted in obedience to Christ. South Africa concerns us all. Every day we read about it in our newspapers. We have mammoth investments there. Many of us have friends and relatives in the country. Above all, for Christians, we have millions of our brothers and sisters in Christ being daily humiliated. This prayer is said daily in Anglican churches in South Africa.

God bless Africa,
Guard her children
Guide her rulers
and give her peace,
For Jesus Christ's sake. Amen

A Theology of the Heart in Russia

I think it was Winston Churchill who described Russia as a mystery inside an enigma inside a mystery. After a short visit there that was certainly my impression. And if it is true of Russia as a whole, it is even more true of the Russian Orthodox Church, whose guest I was. Neverthless it can sometimes be useful to know how other believers cope with such very different situations from our own.

Perhaps the most encouraging fact about the church in Russia is the way young people are being drawn to it. One of the people who looked after me was a good looking young man, in a well-cut suit, who spoke fluent English. Although he was studying for ordination he was married with a one month old daughter, because priests, though not Bishops, are allowed to be married. He was studying theology at one of the church seminaries, at Zagorsk, about 50 miles from Moscow, which I visited. Here there are about 500 students for the priesthood, 350 in the Seminary and 150 doing further theology. I was told that about four or five candidates apply for each available place.

Secondly, one cannot help being impressed by the way the church copes with an avowedly atheistic regime. The Holy Spirit seems to be supplying endless resources of skill and subtlety, courage and sophistication. I was in Moscow for a peace conference of religious leaders from all over the world to talk about how we might contribute to stopping the arms race entering outer space. Of course such a conference only takes place because it is approved by the Soviet Government and serves their purposes. But everything we all do is the result of a mixture of motives. What matters is being aware of what is going on and still trying to bring some good from it. Stopping weapons in space is surely a good – and the church is certainly aware. On Wednesday as we were waiting for the bus to take us to lunch after the morning session, the bus failed to turn up. 'Perhaps we are waiting until they see the results of our morning's work', said one Orthodox. To which another added even more wryly, 'No, until they have evaluated the results of our work – then perhaps the bus will come.' It is an extraordinary situation that the church is trying to live in and coming back I could not help remembering Christ's words, 'Be wise as serpents and harmless as doves.'

And finally, what of the famed spiritual life of the church? Frankly, what I was most immediately aware of was the strong human warmth – the hugs, the kisses, the generous hospitality; but of course all this is underpinned by a deep spirituality. When the monk who showed us round Zagorsk congratulated me on my Russian I protested that I only knew half a dozen words – to which he replied that they had heart in them and that what mattered was 'a theology of the heart'. I liked that: 'A theology of the heart'.

Heavenly Father,
We pray for all believers, wherever they are in
the world,
who are trying to live the life of faith in difficult
circumstances.
Strengthen them and us.

Hope in a Nuclear World

I suppose its characteristic of our mental sleepiness that we accept other people's descriptions of events until they become almost clichés – like calling it a mushroom cloud above the first atomic bomb. A lady once told me she had never liked this description – for she enjoyed mushrooms and liked cooking with them – so she looked at pictures of the cloud again and realised it was not a mushroom at all but a tree. And this reminded us of another tree. You remember that tree in the Garden of Eden, the tree of the knowledge of evil; much to be desired to make one wise? I don't think I have ever really understood that story – why should Adam and Eve have been forbidden to eat the fruit of that tree? But eat they did – and knowledge of all kinds we have had ever since. You may also remember that as a result of eating, Adam and Eve were expelled from Paradise. However much we may long to get back into a state of childlike innocence we can't. We have to live with knowledge, with moral choices – and this includes knowledge of how to make the bomb.

Even the most radical critics of nuclear weapons acknowledge that they cannot now be disinvented. As Jonathan Schell put it: 'Scientific discovery is in this regard like any other form of discovery; once Columbus had discovered America, and had told the world about it, America could not be hidden again.' And alas this means that the threat that nuclear weapons might be used will also be here until the end of time. For even if they were all dismantled but a war broke out both sides could rush to their drawing boards. There is a bit of most of us which hankers after sneaking into the childlike innocence of Eden again, but we have to live with knowledge and the threat it holds out.

Mother Julian of Norwich may in the long run will turn out to be the most distinguished woman this country has ever produced, and a person of ever increasing popularity. Julian, like the rest of us, wondered why God allowed the world to get into such a state; allowed, if you like, such things as nuclear weapons to be invented. She wrote,

'I often wondered why the beginning of sin was not prevented by the great forseeing wisdom of God. But Jesus answered me with this word, saying, 'Sin must needs be, but all shall be well. All shall be well; and all manner of thing shall be well.'

A number of times Julian takes the question back to God – how can this be since there is so much pain, so much suffering? She is not told any detailed answers but time and again those words come back to her. 'It is true that sin is the cause of all this pain. But all shall be well and all shall be well, and all manner of thing shall be well.'

O God, by your divine love we have been created
and by your divine permission we have acquired knowledge of all kinds.
By your divine guidance, lead us through this troubled time.